A Little Style

Rene David Alkalay

This edition published in 2019

The Genesis Society, Inc.

Forest Hills, NY 11375

Copyright © 2019 by The Genesis Society.

All Rights Reserved.

No part of this book may be reproduced, or transmitted in any form or by any means, electronic, or mechanical, including photocopy, without permission in writing from the publisher and author. Reviewers may quote brief passages.

First published in English in 2019.

Rene David Alkalay

A Little Style

ISBN: 978-1-930932-04-3

Other Works by the Same Author:

Kabbalah in Motion: Journeys into Consciousness

Meditation: A Practitioner's Handbook

Meditation and Metaphysical Law: For self-transformation into a Life of Abundance and Joy

The Gentle Path

Sujok Ayurvedic Acupressure

The Darkest Night

Forms

Ghetto Songs and Other Poems

Moon Rites

Past Lives

Contents

Just a Man 5

A Priori – The Egg Dance 7

To Live Now 14

Menage-a-Trois 20

My Mistress 28

A Little Style 30

A Fragrant Gift – a Retro Poem 37

Three Girl-Friends in a Coffee House 39

Love Is All There Is 44

Integrity 47

A Protected Garden 50

A Tentative Beginning 52

The Mind has Questions Part I 54

Fairy Tale – A Retro Poem 58

Sleep My Heart 60

The Marsh 63

When There Were No Shades of Grey 66

You May Believe 68

The Poison Oak 70

Just a Man

Moment by moment, at peace with desire
In her, I awaken in God's renewing fire.
Each kiss is like the ocean's waves on rocks
That break the long forgotten locks.
A touch, a smile, each soft caress
I cannot settle for anything less.

What good are dreams that cannot be
To make her mine yet set her free.
At first I am a warrior on a quest,
A poet witness of the irony and jest,
A king whose weighty kingdom is a test,
A lover in her arms, the very best.

At last when all my journey's done,
I am just a man whose race is not yet run.
Seeing dreams without the old desire
Yet knowing, that, renewed in Godly fire,
Without attachment, I will not let them go,
But grow them in the deeper mind below.

In her, moment by moment, transitions

Briefly, one moment free of definitions

Without attachment, yet without surrender

The warrior's heart is her defender,

The poet sees what words engender,

The king rides forth in kingly splendor,

The lover in her arms so tender.

At last, when my journey's done

I'm just a man turned toward a setting sun.

We whisper love throughout the night

In each other's arms in moonlight.

Seeds dropped in a lovers' bower

In deepest heart begin to flower.

A Priori – The Egg Dance

Let me tell you some clichés about the eggs.

What came first, the chicken or the egg?

To make an omelet you have to break some eggs.

And here's some things you need to know:

When the sun shines, the chicken lays an egg.

Buy eggs from smaller farms and don't trust labels..

Don't whisk, but fork, yes fork.

When scrambling, start with a hot pan.

I've got millions is what she said

And making new ones all the time

A priori - man and woman were around

Hanging out, naked in the garden

They sat under a tree and talked.

Look, the man said, I've got these millions of sperm

The woman replied, that's nice. So what now.

Well, he continued, I'm making 1500 every second.

Okay, she said, so what's your plan, Stan?

I've got an inclination

I've got an inspiration,

I've got determination

I've got motivation and imagination

It sounded good on paper, but they had no clue

They knew the science with no idea what to do.

They tried it straight, they tried it funky,

They tried it standing, and upside down,

They tried it with an orange and with an olive –

The oil felt kind of good – they tried a kiwi

He humped the grass, she humped a tree

They would have given up but for the seer

Who came along and watching all this craziness

Said, look here, that's not the way it goes.

You have to get it hard and put it in her ear.

You can imagine this didn't go too well.

So much for seers.

They kept trying and by some accident

A priori, kids were born and that's how it began.

Now they were caged by schedules,

Trapped in responsibilities.

They diminished into habits and into the mundane

They started wearing clothes.

They were prim and proper.

The man saw bars and fences

The woman saw bars and fences

At night they couldn't stand from tiredness

And so surrendered to blessed sleep.

In the morning she said, this is all your fault

In the afternoon he said, this is all your fault.

At night they were too tired for the blame game.

A priori, eggs the size of grains of sand

And one by one the mass of earth expanded.

It's known but what a mystery

That there are twelve eggs

Just like the signs of the Zodiac,

And then from twelve there's only one.

The signal given, then the push

But life is short so she will say

Hey, big boy, you got what it takes?

The light is faint, so is it fact or fiction?

The garden's past, long gone

Along with play and dance, and song,

But still, it's habitable.

What about Inclination!? None left.

No motivation, no imagination.

1500 sperm every second, all dressed up

And nowhere to go.

Too much ice to break.

I blink and squeeze my eyes shut tight.

I count my breaths.

I tense and release

It just keeps getting worse.

I think I'll change my mind.

I think I'll sleep.

Then morning comes

With morning more bad news.

I know I'm being played but where to go?

Some deserted island. Are there any left?

Deep in the Amazonian jungle? –

I'm no woodsman.

Meditating in a cave in the Himalayas
In the cave monasteries of the great sages -
That is sounding better and better.
But do I have to give up Anger Management?
Can I still watch Seinfeld or Modern Family?
Can I keep watching Game of Thrones, or Gotham?
Can I really give up shopping at Stop and Shop
Or Trader Joe's, or Whole Foods?
Decisions, decisions and choices.

Finally I see a girl with glasses at the public library.
Getting ready to be turned down, I walk up and ask
"Can I have this dance?
She smiles and starts to tell me
About Kepler's Law and Legrange's Point.
I smile and say how very interesting that is
And quickly realize how totally phony I'm being
Because I don't really give a shit about Kepler.
I want to say let's make love right here on this desk
In the public library between the shelves
Of science books and world history.

I want to say I'm looking for my inclination,
My motivation, my imagination.

She sucks me into her world. I feel me slipping
Into friendship and mental masturbation.
I start to tell her about matter and nuclear fusion.
I tell her about conversion of protons to neutrons.
I tell her about the overwhelming noise,
The clatter and the chatter in the universe,
The quasi-stellar objects I have seen
Beyond this galaxy in my imagination
I tell her about retrograde motion and solar cycles.
She looks at me in silence,
She takes her glasses off and asks,
Do you know about eggs?

So it's come around again.
We wake up to cages and fences,
The schedules and responsibilities
The house in the suburbs,
The play dates and social networks,
The right clothes and the family car,

The planned vacations, the family dinners,

Hours of Law and Order SVU and Blue Bloods,

Of Desperate Housewives, and late night hosts,

She wakes up in the morning and says

"This is all your fault."

He call her in the afternoon and says,

"This is all your fault."

And twelve eggs wait and wither,

And 1500 sperm every second get dressed up

And have nowhere to go.

To Live Now

Man

We had a bond. It's not that easy to explain.
As if we came from another time and place
And somehow were brought together again.
There's so many moments that make a life,
So many things in each moment, unexplainable,
Not possible to write or say – the micro-moments
That defy definition, emotions, thoughts,
Becoming sensations, waves of the unknown
That somehow still are so familiar, a laugh,
A smile, a furtive look, an instant boldness,
Distance, fear, a drawing together, the heart
Suddenly speeding up, an emptiness, protection
Raising walls and boundaries, self-destruction.
I see why people call Fate, a fickle goddess.
Whimsical and loving the mischief that she makes
Watching what to us must seem like antics
Of just another fool in the grand scheme of things.
I'll share a thought with you, you may have seen

More likely heard, because the sound reverberates

In every molecule that makes up all that is.

Perhaps we'll talk again and I will share it then.

Woman

No! No! No! Not then. Right now.

You're running.

You know that, right!?

You were abused, hurt,

Treated badly, even cruelly,

And there are moments,

So many moments that make a life.

 I'm laughing.

Do you know why I laugh?

If I stop to think,

Stop to define -

yes, I agree about the indefinite -

So many mistakes that left me down,

Down so far

I wasn't sure I ever could come up,

But I was young.

Even in the darkest life,

There's something to be said,

Something about being young

Youth's exuberance and hope.

But how many times can you get up?

Slap me down!

Slap me down again.

Fight me. Rip my clothes off.

Love me, hate me,

But don't run away and hide.

I need you to stand up,

Be strong, yes, be heroic.

Be the dream I thought

I couldn't dream again.

Man

Okay, most of the best moments never need words.

The best of those were when the babies came.

Each year, each day, each minute, each moment

My voice became more powerful and I fought.

I was the knight who slew the dragon,

I was the wizard casting rings of protection,

I was the shaman mixing magic potions.

There never was a shortage of heartache,

And all those turbulent nights,

Oh yes, the nights when sleep wouldn't come,

Worry about tomorrow, about enough food,

Decisions of where to live,

Without selling my soul,

Without selling my body

As something to be beaten,

Without offering my heart for trampling.

Is that why I understand?

Why we are here and now,

That I can recognize in your eyes what I've known?

I'll stop running. I'll stay. You can hold my heart.

There's different ways to die.

Some die and are gone.

What if we die and have to stay?

Nothing left to give,

Empty inside, our vision seeing flat colors

Beautiful sounds meaningless,

smiles and greetings returned as surfaces,

Only less than actors on a stage.

Woman

I've got a plan. Let's live, not die.

This is day one.

Each day we'll bless the time we have,

Each moment, another chance

To make it right.

A day that we can drop the games,

Be naked to our very core.

 Is that a possibility?

I don't know, but I can never hurt you,

You are my mate, my friend, my husband

For that very knife I were to plunge in you

Would pierce two hearts,

And both would cease to be.

We do philosophize,

But there's still time.

Beyond the game of time there is beyond the game,

Beyond the words, to know that we are one.

In us the same divinity resides,

A divinity waiting to be awakened.

Menage-a-Trois

I am silken and white

As the inside of a women's thighs.

I am as black as the onyx

That comes from the fire,

I am as pink as the lips I have kissed

At times, I am, as sages often are,

Free of all desire.

By memory or imagination,

I don't know which,

I walked in the first garden

Walked with an Adam and an Eve,

With them I tasted the pleasures,

Those of the mind and those of the flesh

Yet I questioned all that I believed.

We were the only three

We gave birth to all who came after.

They called me serpent,

Satan, the fallen one,

He who tempted woman

To forget her wedding vows,

Black and hard as onyx,

White as the blinding sun,

I am Venus, I am the rising star

By memory or imagination,

My child was born,

Emerging from, what seemed to me,

The blackest hole

Tied to harpies and furies,

Creatures without a soul.

My downfall in the end

Was fear born of ignorance

I had no patience

For the woman or her man

I thought how foolish

How fallible they are

And questioned once again

If there ever was a plan.

I overcame disgust at such a dirty creature

Whenever the Adam left to gather wheat and corn

She called to me, and leaving reason, I would go

And so it happened that a second son was born.

Somewhere deep inside,

I felt a pressure on my chest.

I was as cold as earth

My curse to slither in the dust.

I couldn't rise, not face her,

Not look into her eyes

The iron in my blood became a useless rust.

I am as silken and white

As the inside of a woman's thighs

I am as black as the onyx

That comes from the fire.

In memory I am as pink

As the lips I have kissed

In imagination I am, as sages often are,

Free of desire.

It was determined after all

That the Adam have a mate

To help him plough

The vaginal field of his Eve

To teach what already was in man from birth

To lust and cheat, to kill, to lie and to deceive.

I gave birth to all who were before

And to all who are now

Caged and shackled for this travesty

I hide from light and seek the night,

The solace of murky shadows.

Seeking liberation, I know that I'm not free.

This Genesis is long gone, fact or fiction,

Memory or imagination, where is the lie?

Her heart was broken when I turned away

She reasoned her perfection,

And that the fool therefore was I.

In her eyes the serpent fell and she had sons.

Why spoil her dream

Why tell her what is yet to come.

I have no inclination,

Neither wanting or not wanting.

I sit alone in a vast wasteland

Beating on a drum.

What is it that disturbs my peace?

Simply that I don't know why.

What is the point?

Only the dead sand can hear.

Only imagined purity and silence,

Fictional peace and tranquility

Sometimes, unexpectedly,

There is an occasional tear.

I have not tasted woman's lips or fondled breasts.

I have not sought to die between a woman's thighs.

Wealth and power seem like just another game

That little boys will play when getting high.

I wanted to believe the world

Would be a saner place,

I wanted to be wrong about the future,

To not see what I had seen beyond today.

Perhaps to change the world

By the power of my will.

I am as silken and white

As the inside of a woman's thighs

I am as black as the onyx

That comes from the fire.

In memory I am as pink

As the lips I have kissed

In imagination I am, as sages often are,

Free of desire.

I couldn't tell what I'd seen,

The broken bones

The blood stained fields,

The rotting flesh,

The stare of unbelieving eyes,

The heart of man

That's made of stone.

I saw it in the foulness of the blackest hole

Home of harpies and furies come to earth.

For higher love I ran,

Knowing this would be misunderstood

For higher love I wanted no part

In any more birth, wanted freedom from fear.

My steel is melted, my armor and rust are gone

I'm sick of war, I'm tired of war,

Immortal, I have no thought of death.

Yet in the forms, I am a metal soldier,

A soldier made of fragile breath

And Sometimes, unexpectedly,

There is an occasional tear.

I am as silken and white

As the inside of a woman's thighs

I am as black as the onyx

That comes from the fire.

In memory I am as pink

As the lips I have kissed

In imagination I am, as sages often are,

Free of desire.

My Mistress

Awake! Awake! Let warm winds blow.

Let cooling streams and river's rush

Awake, my world of green, my child that in me stirs

And Venus be my goddess

My mistress of the moon, my cypress trees,

Awake my dove of peace,

The moon is crescent in a honeyed land.

My mistress, her staff in hand,

Her triangle of power at the heart

And down below, the new flower.

Awake! Awake! Dance on golden sheaths of wheat

Disappear in lover's arms and passion's heat

You are my shield of peace on your bench of stone

And cypress trees surround you my Queen of love,

High mountain streams feed the honeycomb

Our marriage bed consummate, apart, alone

There, by the stream and by the waterfall,

The child begins its downward journey.

It is the fruit and the growth
And twelve stars guide the infant's fall.

You are my golden wheat, my heart, my dove.
Your hand holds potencies from powers above.
My preservation, my protection is your love
Diffuse me into molecules of perpetual dance
Transmit me to the universe.
Dissolve me into your creative thought.

Awake, my mistress of the field and wood.
Awake, my cypress trees,
Awake, and take me through
Your door of thoughts and moods.
Awake, from slumber in your frozen land,
From stones and sleeping holly
We touch and in your eyes, my constancy
Shifts from wisdom to my happiest folly.

A Little Style

Everyone I talk to is looking

For just that perfect one.

We wish for Mr. Right,

We wish for Ms Right

And we overlook the rest.

In the club, the music plays,

And blondes are everywhere.

In shopping malls there's redheads,

There's purple heads and blue.

There's raven headed beauties

Parading through the streets

But I have found

That I never notice brown haired girls.

I thought I must be brain-washed.

And all those women

With push-up bras and perky breasts

And women in their forties

In the bars with loose tea shirts

With blood-shot eyes, braless and floppy.
After one more beer she said,
"Got to let my girls breathe."

Chic, latest fashion clothes,
Tory Burch country club ready.
I saw one girl that walked on stilts, or so I thought.
Then enlightenment,
They were just Maison Margiela Lifted Loafers.
She stood there with her friend
On Square Toed Stompers.

Then I saw her, a brunette
With a Jeremy Scott I-phone case,
Proenza Schouler's door knockers
Impossible to miss.
I see you but you're everywhere and so
I don't really see you,
Not even with Altuzarra's cherry red hoops

Out goes Louis Vutton,

And in with monogrammed leather.

I joined the club so, yes,

It's time for me to confess.

It was one freezing day in March,

About two years ago,

I spent all night waiting in a line of guys,

Waiting and for what?

Was it to hear Kendrick Lamar,

or Bruno Mars, or Old Dominion?

Would I get to see Cardi B

Strutting her stuff or hear Demi Lovato?

Oh, I was definitely in the in-crowd

And when it was my turn

I shelled out 300 bucks on Orchard Street

For my Nike Pigeon Dunks.

When I got home you'd think

I thought that I was nuts? No way!

Going down to Nom de Guerre

And get those Slim Shady Nikes

Now let me try to explain.

The others, they were mostly kids.

But have you ever seen this real old guy

In his red convertible.

Ever wonder what that's about?

Well, like redheads and blondes,

Like purple haired girls and brunettes,

They come in different colors.

Now I'm looking for Gucci sweaters

And the layerable, versatile shirt.

My next move is all in black denim.

I like my convertible because

It makes me feel like nothing else can.

I like my convertible because

I feel the wind rushing through my hair.

I like my convertible because

It gives me that rush in my belly

That I sometimes forget is still there,

Those embers sparking into fire.

Oh, I finally deprogrammed myself
About all the shit that's going down.
The radical left and the radical right,
The skin heads, the Nazis and the communists,
The health care crisis, the immigrants,
The dreamers and the wall,
The pro-Trumpers and the anti-Trumpers,
Everything I thought was real,
The end of the world
With nukes flying and armies clashing,

The babies crying and mothers grieving,
The hungry and homeless,
The women raped and beaten,
The rows of old people in hallways
In nursing homes sitting
With glazed eyes and mindless stares
And hope that someone will visit,
That someone will remember their name,

Women with memories
Of when they were blondes and redheads

Or raven haired beauties

parading through the streets, -

The brown haired girl who was,

You guessed it, my perfect match -

When men's head's turned

And men's eyes undressed them,

How they felt in their Cinnamon Scones Heels

And their Baby dolls,

Their Polka Dot Madden

And their Hepcat Soda Fountain.

Oh yes, they turned my head with their Suit skirts,

With their pattern blouses and cardigans.

The old men sat in wheelchairs in the hallways,

Grumpy and stubborn,

They remembered chasing the girl

I in her Sailor Pants Denim

They remembered the Voodoo Vixen

With her Marilyn Pumps.

It was fun to think of how

To get a girl out of all those great clothes.

The old men remembered

Their Converse Classic All Star sneakers

Their grey, pin-striped suits,

Their Felt Fedora, and their red convertibles.

Oh yeah, I finally deprogrammed myself

About all the shit that's going down.

It's like it always was. The killing doesn't end

But we will have our little style

A Fragrant Gift – a Retro Poem

As I walked in my garden one day
I found a flower with her petals closed
"It must have been the wind," I thought,
"That's placed this flower near my way."

Drawn to her, I stepped away
From my well-worn path to see
This strange addition I'd not sown
Nor having seen before this day.

I sat before her in deepest thought
And slowly came to love the core
Of what the petals could not hide,
A sweet fragrance we've always sought.

Looking closely I could also see
Some bruising on the stems and roots
So, bringing mulch for root to take
I sought to set this flower free.

Her petals opened to the sun

She drank the water that I gave

Released her fragrance as a gift

And she and I were one.

With season's change, she's gone away

For she was always free

But she has left her fragrant gift

Of seeds to blossom on another day.

Three Girl-Friends in a Coffee House

First Friend

Should we keep silent in the face of disrespect?.

Doesn't our silence lower us all?

And if we speak, what is the risk?

A chance maybe to lose a friend.

But then what friend would act this way?

No! we can't be silent. Not today.

We'll speak out, and from the heart

And if it's meant to be that friendships part

We'll speak no matter how it ends.

Second Friend

How vulnerable we are to those that we let in.

Discovering how hard it is to trust,

A trust misplaced In those whose passion is to win

Greater than their caring about what's lost.

So, yes, I understand this separation,

This going inward, this isolation.

Work is pure until we look for some relation.

The world around us drags us down
To be an adjective when we want to be a noun.

Third Friend

Yes! How easy it is to close the heart,
To sleep and let the days pass by,
Forget to laugh, forget to cry,
Even think that we might keep
Our dignity intact, but no! Let's speak
Though it will be that by that speech
We are pulled down. We may impeach
Those that are usually out of reach.
I think we always seek what's true
And risk our hearts with just a few.

First Friend

There's no denying we'd rather stand alone.
I think some trap is always set
From high up on some celestial throne
Before we can receive, to pay a debt
We have no knowledge of, nor ever had.

My first lover was a little mad

Still I never thought it would be bad.

He left me and I never said a word.

I thought my silence would be heard.

Second Friend

There's only so many times our hearts can break.

I fear to pin my hopes on anyone.

Pushed to the edge of how much to take,

I can't see clearly and so I continuing to run.

I will not sleep my days and nights away

Nor wait expecting some perfect day.

By action and design, all my fears allay

I know my tolerance for risk is low

I have no clue of what to do or where to go.

Third Friend

Mine was a friend since we were kids.

It was a rainy day. No-one was home.

I knew that it was something they'd forbid.

We found the Kama sutra. We chanted Ohm.
We bowed to one another, followed the text,
By mutual choice, we turned to what came next.
Since I chose, I never was perplexed.
Silence, fantasy, and all our expectations
Serve slightly, but not as well as clear intentions.

Second Friend

There's someone now, a married man.
I thought that with the knowing, it couldn't last,
It gave me safety. It would be my best plan
To leave my deepest feelings in the past.
Enjoy the time we have, not wanting more,
I said, and shun the weakness I abhor,
Or play the game of love I've played before.
It hasn't worked as I thought it would.
I wait and hope that it will not be good.

First Friend

What you've said may be the reason

We cannot speak, although we must.

This year I do expect the rainy season,

Alone to contemplate on who to trust.

Love Is All There Is

The universe is lazy, so I've read,
Planets moving slowly on their course,
At times, a shooting star speeds ahead
All reflections of a hidden source.

Black holes, born of dying stars,
More numerous than grains of sand,
Hold all imprisoned behind bars.
This too then, by a guiding Hand.

So we must be to keep the pace
To hold the rhythm and the rhyme
Neither run from place to place
Nor be the whim of man-made time.

Our strategy, to see the board,
Before the pieces we are played
On which we cut the birthing cord
And all our options have been weighed.

Here we are then, you and I,

Part slave, part master of our destiny.

A center between earth and sky,

Imprisoned light that's rarely free.

Until, at last, we break the ties,

Surrender flesh to waiting arms,

Drift lazily into a dark beyond

That light may thus begin to rise.

There is another way, an urge

That drives us on to love

Open arms with which to merge

Ourselves to that which is above.

Here too, a fearless spirit is found,

That dares to seek beyond the broken parts,

Holding truth as new, discovered ground

Challenging our wounded hearts.

Come with me where the mind may go

Leave what is hers and what is his,

Leave heaven above and earth below

True or false, Love's all there is.

Integrity

Integrity is a much used word,
The plaything of the common herd
Too often just the service of lips
Forgotten easily with the shake of hips
And vows that were in passion made
Have not the weight of getting laid.

It's not another that can break the heart
But always choice that makes us part.
No time for tears or wanting more
When fear has rotted out the core
And three strikes granted for love's sake
But there's no fourth that we can make.

For in that making we are undone
By our own choosing to be the one
In self-deception to remain
The composer of our pain.
Better by far to walk away
And love again another day.

Easy then to bow our head
In service to the heart, it's said
But it was never meant to be,
That we submit to tyranny,
The uninstructed heart at best
Renouncing reason and mind's rest.

Thus let the heart choose the dream
And reason be the lighthouse beam
That guides us safely to our home
Without that beacon, the heart will roam
On hidden reefs to surely crash.
Recall the drum and take the cash.

So, this night will also pass
The many thoughts that now harass,
That steal a night of peaceful sleep,
These will sink into the deep
This very night we may be sad
With that which drives so many mad.

What use to curse what seems so bad

Can there be gain in what we had?

Fearless, face loss as a friend

Not truth, but love with reason as the end

Not words, in wars that can't be won

For by the heart alone we are undone.

A Protected Garden

Dreams are fragile things mainly made of fairy dust

Every dreamer has his Tinker Bell to point the way

Fairyland's a special place where iron never rusts

Where all is ever fresh and there is no decay

Where all can be as fast as we can think or say.

The fear to dream is that with morning we awake

And dreams take flight

Forgotten with the morning light.

It's not the dream we fear

But that the heart may break

If we lose reason and relinquish inner sight,

If we invest ourselves once more in the night.

But, what's the choice? Shall we settle into reason?

Each day another endless set of measured steps

Can it be rebellion, or even treason

To venture where the creatures of myth are kept.

What is the Garden that we so carefully protect?

A Tentative Beginning

Asleep on your pillow, your hair in a mess
I'm feeling what words can never express
The years we're together have gone so fast
This day's a chance to lose the past

Our children are grown, the cat has died
Now we'll see if the others have lied
Now we can let our lives begin
See who we can be, leave who we've been

If I can help your dreams come true
Gray hair and years would fall away
Perhaps I haven't told you how we grew
Together and how we wrote our play

The unwritten chapters yet to come,
Like Khayam's distant drum,
Are the mystery that lies ahead
And you sleep peaceful in our bed.

I haven't slept this whole night through

For this need to think of you

The many paths we've yet to tread

The many times to still break bread

And you may think the bird of youth

Has nested in another's truth

And even think how time has fled-

For now, forgotten in our bed.

The Mind has Questions - Part I

The mind has questions for love in the light of day
Shall I let all reason fly away,
Surrender heart and soul, give all I have,
In innocence, offering a sacrificial calve
Offered to a capricious god or goddess.
Is that not one of the many forms of madness?

Is reason not the better way, once seen?
Yet, can the reasoning mind ever be truly green?
Is birth a new beginning or an end
When what is final is that we cannot mend?
If God is getting high on pot
Am I allowed to laugh, or not?

The mind has questions for love in the light of day.
By moonlight there's very little I need to say.
Surrender heart and soul to waiting arms
Suspend my disbelief for a moment's charms.
Must I then agree that day is ample reason
For gates to close upon my growing season?

What hazy thoughts, and how short-sighted

To thus allow the mind, uninvited,

Envisioning pictures of what I fear the most,

To take command as if it were the host

And I, a guest, by what I hold most dear -

The adventure of an unexplored frontier.

The mind has questions for love in the light of day.

The questions are the price to pay

For what must surely be a priceless gift

That is our anchor when our ship's adrift.

Must I then chart the given points on graphs

Or see, in the mind's shadows, a god who laughs?

The Mind Has Questions - Part II

I have questions for love in the light of day

Last night was magic, the feel of you

Your smell intoxicated me, your eyes

Were like great orbs of onyx

With the molten fire of the volcano.

Your skin was silk, your laugh was dulcet.

I woke up with you in my bed,
Your hair disheveled, parched lips.

The make-up gone, the blemished skin
Moving closer, against my inclination,
A morning kiss, your breath a fearful thing
And behind the fire in your eyes

I saw the cold stillness of the grave.
An hour in the bathroom
And last night YOU were back
A vision of delight, a flower garden
From second impressions of Horror Story
To the intoxication of "It's a Wonderful Life."
Breakfast at the diner, nothing could be finer.

We went to Central Park, I held your hand
The first few minutes of our first morning
Were gone and I couldn't help thinking
About reality and illusion, about what is so
And what I want things to be,
the dream We dream with open eyes

At times dreading what we might see

With the coming of the light.

Should I let reason simply rule,

Never give my heart and soul

Never live the moment of my death

Nor hear the laughter of capricious gods?

So what's the choice -

Let reason go and live the dream?

One is cold as ice,

A northern wind that chills the soul.

The other is an unchecked flame,

A fire that devours the living wood.

I know there is another way.

I hope there is another way.

Fairy Tale – A Retro Poem

So, here I am, imaginary prince

Of all the fairy tales my mother read

Of all the heroes I have been since

In films and books, and fears that I have shed

To face the fiery dragons that I dread.

The damsel in her tower waits for me

One like the sun that brings the warmth of day

Another like the moon's dark mystery

And I, the hero, in my story's play

Discover that I may be an old cliché.

No damsel in her tower waits for me

The sun now passes through polluted layers

The moon is hardly any mystery

The field is not for heroes, but players

And very little on which we can agree.

Sleep My Heart

Sleep my heart, be at peace, unwind.

How, when there is no peace of mind?

How easily the words of love are spoken.

Equally easy the vows of love are broken.

Knowing this is little consolation

For exchanging love for the safety of separation.

Sleep my heart, who knows when you will wake?

Until then be the mirror of my silent lake

Without a ripple in the stillness at dusk

Release for now the heavy scent of musk

That can so quickly overpower all sense

To trick us into planning in a future tense.

Sleep my heart, I know that you can heal

Acknowledge, but step back, from what you feel.

Go into silence where rests the golden balm

That protects us from a greater harm

On fresh made wounds, gathered and placed

That wounds may heal and only scars are traced.

Sages have long taught to empty our cup

Before we join them at evening to sup.

Here in the silence I have found all the parts,

The scattered pieces of eons of broken hearts,

Woven into a rainbow tapestry

We try to build into remembered harmony.

Sleep my heart, be at peace and rest.

Loss comes inevitably as a test

Calm and silence are shaken by the musky scent

We give freely that which others sell or rent

When love has gone and we are left to mend

A slight wisdom gained to our self to tend.

The Marsh

Naked in my arms, her fragrance unmistakable,

Firm skin of youth, white as egrets in a marsh,

A dark goddess, her salty lips were things of fable.

Vulnerable, thus unforgiving, at times too harsh

When that which is submerged is taken to the light.

In her saturation, supported, all stand firm

Absorbing strength, transported to the deep

The broad leaved plants and the hot spent sperm.

And I, with foolish pride, have made her weep

The goddess thus retreated to the darkest night.

Laughter in her eyes, the smallest word was home

Youth wades and fishes in the saturated marsh.

The goddess awakened,

The goddess, progeny of the marsh foam,

Hears egrets' croaking sounds and calls too harsh

For hearts and limbs entwined in passion's flame

Roots redundant but for anchorage in this world,

Submerged leaves not wanting to emerge on land.

Without choice, the child that lies so curled

Inside the warmth and safety of her womb,

Although by fate was planned,

Surely will emerge to change

The nature of the game.

Naked in my arms, so many years gone their way,

The grasses, weeds, and sedges of the marsh

Are fragrant as they were when first we played.

In the heart these years have never been so harsh

That with the dryness of the wetlands

Could ever hide the deeper waters,

A home to water lilies and wild rice,

White as the egrets that continue to return,

A dark goddess, whose skin of late

Adorned with spice,

Takes from the marsh

The fire that continues to burn

In eyes within whose depths

I see a youthful bride.

When There Were No Shades of Grey

Chorus

You feed my body with a kiss

You feed my mind with dreams

I remember things I've missed

Times when all extremes

Were reachable each day

And nothing was in shades of grey.

You fed my thoughts with words

My feelings flowed from mountain tops

Now world is forever blurred

The seeds, they grow unfamiliar crops

The middle path that was my day

By light of moon have passed away.

Above me I can see a hawk

That circles searching for its prey

Below me are the building blocks

That draw me to an old cliché.

Round and round my reason goes

Seeking anchors that I chose.

Awake, I thus renew a quest

Left by a road, I don't know where

Not wanting what I left behind

Thoughts within a troubled mind.

Heart open now, you feed my soul

Revealing parts I thought were whole.

Chorus

You feed my body with a kiss

You feed my mind with dreams

I remember things I've missed

Times when all extremes

Were reachable each day

And nothing was in shades of grey.

You May Believe

Run as fast and far as ever you can
It's fear that's chasing you now
You've landed in the frying pan
The question never was why, but how.
I, an untrained actor, missing cues
Have birthed the fear that we would lose

It's fear that I can't keep her long
Or give her all the things she needs.
But if I still can sing that ancient song
And see the flowers past the weeds
Then I will care for her through time
And reassure her that she's mine.

In thought we're never far apart.
It is a dream that we have dreamt,
A dream that somewhere in the heart
The spoken words were really meant.
She is afraid to trust and ache
Not again to let the heart break.

Who can blame her then, not I.

My own heart knows just what she feels.

To sit alone and then to cry

For what she thought might just be real.

Be brave, have courage, I will not leave.

By actions, not by words, you may believe.

The Poison Oak

Many things in every corner of the earth,
Bald eagle searched, and then he spoke
So, from clay, man had his birth
From a feather by man, a woman awoke
The man slept on by a poison oak

To flapping wings the man then stirred
And woman felt the tightening yoke
Above them, flying off, the bird
Had left them to what seemed a joke
To make children by a poison oak.

Built up village then became a town,
Until earth and tree began to choke
No space where Bald Eagle could set down
No air to fly that's clear of smoke,
Just one small place by a poison oak.

This collection of poetry has offered me a wonderful opportunity for self-growth. As much as I have enjoyed reading these poems, I have equally, if not more so, been strongly moved by Dr. Rene's reading of his work. Listening to him, I have found someone who not only hears me, but has managed to express so many of my own thoughts about things. Thank you, Dr. Rene   Josephine, B., Hillside, NY

The work of Dr. Rene is both poetry and drama, high-brow, classical, retro, and whimsical all in one. The many characters that are throughout these poems could easily be the cast of a play, or many plays. I've enjoyed the poems for their sense of sincerity and their facilitating an exploration of solutions and opportunities for living.   Alan, B., Provincetown, RI

Exciting! Wonderful! Stimulating! Loved all of the poems and keep quoting them to friends.
JoAnn, M., Croton-on-the-Hudson, NY

Sat in on a reading. Thanks for sharing your wisdom. I especially liked your retro poems.   Lemark, J., Brooklyn, NY

This is the fourth book of poetry of yours that I have. Each one has moved me and helped me to see things from a new perspective. I'm looking forward to the next one. I hope it will be soon.   Rhonda, S., Pheonix, AZ

www.ingramcontent.com/pod-product-compliance
Lightning Source LLC
LaVergne TN
LVHW091319080426
835510LV00007B/558